Steve,

Here's some fun, creative ideas of things we can do together for our next 32 years.

Happy 32nd Anniversary...

♡ U,

Becky

2-15-09

To:

Steve

from:

Bechy

Published by Hallmark Books, a division of Hallmark Cards, Inc., under license from Howard Books, a division of Simon & Schuster, Inc.

Hallmark Books, a division of Hallmark Cards, Inc.
Kansas City, MO 64141

Visit us on the web at www.Hallmark.com.

Art Director: Kevin Swanson
Designer: Myra Colbert Design
Production Artist: Dan C. Horton

ISBN: 978-1-59530-013-3

BOK4355

Printed and bound in China

It's a Date!

52 ways

to have fun
TOGETHER

GIFT BOOKS
from Hallmark

Introduction

You try to plan fun dates — dates that let the two of you spend time together having fun and growing your relationship. But where do you go and what do you do? Have your dates become a little "been there, done that"?

If that sounds like you and your special someone, this little book could be just what you need. Inside, there are 52 suggestions for date night (one for each week). Many are inexpensive or cost nothing at all. Others will require you to plan carefully and put some money away ahead of time. There are fun dates, reflective dates, extreme dates, dates that focus on conversation — all kinds of dates. Each one contains a little romance and a lot of fun.

Discover great ideas to maximize your time together, and learn how to get out of the "dinner-and-a-movie" rut. Are you ready to see how much fun dating can be?

Create a Masterpiece

Explore your creative side with a fun, lighthearted art project. Get out some finger paints and a large piece of paper, and see what you can create together. You could agree to do a picture of something in particular or go completely abstract. Or you could pick up a paint-by-number picture and have fun working on the design together. While you're waiting for your masterpiece to dry, go to the store and find the perfect frame to display your work so you can preserve this special memento of the fun you have as a couple.

BUDGET

$ The art supplies for these projects are inexpensive, and you may already have some supplies around the house. You can even make your own finger paints. Recipes are available online.

OVER THE TOP

- Take an art class together. There are lots of options — oil painting, watercolor, pottery, mosaics, and many others.
- Visit an art museum for inspiration. Some museums will even allow you to take your art supplies along and work on your project on the museum grounds.
- Eat at a restaurant that displays local talent.

GET CONNECTED

- Key search words: finger paints, paint by number, art classes, art museums

number
2

Heads Up!

A new spin on the old miniature golf standby is disc golf. It's played with specially designed Frisbees, and most cities have parks that are equipped for this sport. Best of all, after your initial investment in a few discs, it's free to play and can provide hours of fun in the great outdoors. Discs can be purchased at most sporting goods stores. There are almost as many different kinds of discs as there are golf clubs, but a couple of multipurpose discs and maybe a putter are all you'll need to get started. You don't need to be particularly athletic or coordinated to play. Just have fun. It's a great way to get some exercise and to talk your loved one into going to the park if he or she isn't particularly interested in romantic walks. Keep score if you want, and maybe even agree on a prize for the winner. But don't let the competition overshadow your true goal of spending time together and growing closer. If you're both highly competitive, you may want to agree on a handicap system so each of you has an equal chance of winning.

BUDGET

$–$$ The cost will go up if you have to buy a disc.

WHAT TO TAKE

- Disc
- Water bottles
- Running shoes

STEPS TO SUCCESS

- Know the rules but don't let them get in the way of fun.

OVER THE TOP

- Pack a romantic picnic lunch including items such as deli meats, cheese, crackers, fruit, and a decadent dessert. Some sparkling grape juice or cider is also a nice addition.

- Visit the park ahead of time, and leave some love notes at a few of the holes (nothing too personal since other golfers may see them first).

GET CONNECTED

- If you are a novice, check out **everythingdisc.com** for rules and beginner disc recommendations.

- There's even a video game version at **miniclip.com/discgolf.htm.**

- Key search words: disc, golf followed by your city and state

Romance Her

They say "diamonds are a girl's best friend,"
but there is one thing she will cherish even more —
a love letter from her sweetheart. Find some pretty
paper, and simply pour out your heart.
Tell her how much she means to you and those things
you love most about her. Whether your note is long
or relatively short, you'll knock the ball out of the
park with this one.

number
3

Music Makes the World Go 'Round

Do you love rock and roll, or is jazz more your style? Whatever your musical taste, a concert can be a great place to let loose and enjoy some time together doing something out of the ordinary. If you both enjoy the same types of music, pick an artist or group you both love. If your musical tastes differ, each of you should choose a concert you'd like to go to. If you can, attend both. If not, flip a coin to decide whose pick to go with. Regardless of who wins the coin toss, join in and have fun as if you're the group's biggest fan.

BUDGET

$$ Prices will vary depending on the location of the seats and the popularity of the artist. For an inexpensive date, look for a free outdoor concert in your area.

OVER THE TOP

- Make the evening more memorable by splurging on front row seats or backstage passes.

GET CONNECTED

- If you have a specific artist or group in mind, visit their Web site for concert information.
- Key search words: concerts, bands followed by your city and state

number
4

Old-Fashioned Hayride

Organize an old-fashioned hayride for the two of you —
or invite a few other romantically inclined couples to join
you. Before you get started, to get yourself in the mood,
rake some leaves on a crisp, golden, autumn day. When
you've got the biggest pile you can possibly make, hold
hands and take a running leap right onto it. Lie down and
gaze up at the blue sky and puffy clouds, just as you did
when you were kids.

BUDGET

$$ Relatively inexpensive

WHAT TO TAKE

- Warm clothing and blankets
- Fixings to make s'mores

STEPS TO SUCCESS

- Be sure to wear warm, layered clothing that can be added or removed easily as the weather dictates.

OVER THE TOP

- End the hayride at a bonfire with a great grilled dinner waiting.
- Take along a CD player with your favorite guitar music to enjoy with the bonfire.

GET CONNECTED

- Key search words: horses, hayride, horse ranch

What a grand thing,
to be loved!
What a grander thing still,
to love!

VICTOR HUGO

Picnicking Under the Stars

What could be more romantic than a night sky? That's easy: two lovers out under it! For a date that will put stars in your eyes, try the following ideas:

- Picnic under the stars at twilight.
- As the sky deepens, learn the constellations and point them out to each other.
- If you picnic during July or August, you may be able to witness the Perseid meteor shower.
- Look for shooting stars, and make wishes on them.
- Contemplate the harvest moon.
- Cuddle in a sleeping bag for two as twilight turns to velvety darkness.

BUDGET

$ Food for the picnic

WHAT TO TAKE

- Picnic blanket and supplies
- Warm clothing
- Sleeping bags (or a bag for two)

STEPS TO SUCCESS

- Check the weather.
- Pick a field or meadow outside of town with an unimpeded view of the sky. Be sure it is a safe place.

OVER THE TOP

- Take a deck of cards or board game and play by flashlight.
- Consider visiting your local planetarium. After the show, go outside and see if you can name the stars or locate a constellation.
- Discuss the universe and our world on the drive home. Watch out — this could lead to an even deeper discussion about the meaning of life.

GET CONNECTED

- Key search words: planets, stars, constellations, planetariums, universe

Trip Down Memory Lane

What do you remember most about the day you and your sweetheart first met? How about your first date? For a fun, nostalgic date, see if you can re-create the moment you first met or your first date. See how much you can remember, and try to get the details as close to the original as possible. Do you remember what you each were wearing? If you don't have the same clothes anymore, see if you can find something similar. If you went out to eat or to a movie or ball game on your first date, try to arrange to sit in the same seats. Were other friends or family members involved in your meeting? Why not include them in the fun and see if they'd like to help you re-create the moment you met? Whether this date is simple or elaborate, have a great time refreshing your memories of an important milestone in your love story.

BUDGET

$–$$$ The amount you spend on this date will depend on how elaborate you choose to get or on what you did on your first date. If you've moved away and can't afford the traveling expenses to return to the original location, see if you can find someplace similar nearby.

GET CONNECTED

- Go online to check the current status of locations you'd like to revisit, to order tickets to a movie or event, or to find specific items to make your reenactment more authentic.

Visit a Retro Roller Rink

Sure, it might conjure up images of junior high, with all the nervousness and sweaty palms that came with the "couples' skate," but good old-fashioned roller skating is not only fun, it's a great workout! Nowadays, many people have traded in their roller skates for the more modern, outdoor Rollerblades™, but for a fun (and heart-pounding) date idea, nothing beats the roller rink. Imagine it — the music, the sound of wheels on wood, skaters leaning into the turns and then picking up the pace on the straightaways. It's magical. And if you're lucky, you might even get to hold that special someone's hand under the disco ball.

BUDGET

$$ Most roller-skating rinks have inexpensive entrance fees, but you'll also need to cover refreshments and skate rentals — for two.

STEPS TO SUCCESS

- Have you forgotten how to roller skate or never really learned? Here are easy, no-fail steps to get you moving around the rink in no time.

Step 1: Place your feet in a "V" position, with your heels together and your toes apart.

Step 2: Keep your body upright, and don't look down!

Step 3: Bend your knees slightly, and stretch your arms out for balance.

Step 4: Begin to "march," not walk, using small baby steps. Lift your knees, keeping your feet in the "V" position.

Step 5: Don't attempt to slide your skates. If your feet stay in the correct place, your skates will roll.

Step 6: When you are ready for it, push your skate out to the side. This will get you moving forward.

- If you are feeling ambitious, try skating backward — with the flow of traffic, of course. Skate just as you would going forward, except keep your toes together and your heels apart, in an inverse "V" position.

OVER THE TOP

- Buy your own roller skates or buy a pair for your sweetie.
- Rent the roller-skating rink for the night for just the two of you. Provide the deejay with a CD of your date's favorite songs ahead of time. Be sure to include some fun and funky tunes as well as some romantic ones to set the mood.

GET CONNECTED

- To find a roller-skating rink in your area, check out **seskate.com/rinks.**
- Key search words: roller skate, rinks, how to skate

Romance Him

Tell your florist you want to send your man flowers
at the office. Women send men flowers all the time
these days, and your florist will know just how
to arrange and package them for maximum masculine
appeal. He might act a little embarrassed at first,
but he won't be able to hide the smile.
Don't forget to attach a romantic note.

The Great Cookie Hunt

See if you can find the best cookie in your city. Visit local bakeries, the cookie shop at your local mall — anyplace you can think of that makes good cookies. You'll probably want to sample just a bite or two of each cookie and then take the rest home to enjoy later so you don't end your date early with an upset stomach! If you can't agree on just one winner, you could each rank them from your favorite to least favorite and see which cookie shows up toward the top of each of your lists. This activity could be especially fun during the Christmas season when there will be additional holiday selections to choose from, and you just may find the perfect treat to take to holiday parties.

BUDGET

$ Cookies are usually a fairly inexpensive treat.

OVER THE TOP

- See if you can come up with your own original cookie recipe, and give it a sentimental name that has something to do with your love story.
- Spend the evening baking your recipe together.

Love consists in desiring
to give what is our own to another
and feeling his delight
as our own.

EMANUEL SWEDENBORG

number 9

Test-Drive Your Dream Car

When you hear the words dream car, what image springs to mind? If it's the latest minivan with the perfect setup for a family, try thinking a little further — beyond what's practical to something that's just plain fun. What about the shiny sports car he's dreamed of driving since he was a little boy? Or maybe the snazzy convertible she pictured herself in during college? Decide what it is you're looking for, and then head to the car lot for a test-drive. Even if your dream car is destined to remain in the realm of fantasy, you can still have a great time checking out the car lots and sharing your dream with each other.

BUDGET

$ A test-drive won't cost you anything, but if you're prone to impulse buying, you may want to leave your checkbook and credit cards at home!

OVER THE TOP

- Rent your dream car for the weekend and take it on a road trip, or rent it when you get to your destination and have a blast driving it around town.
- If your dream car is something you'd both honestly like to own someday, why not set up a separate savings account and start working toward that goal a little at a time?

GET CONNECTED

- Get online to find a dealership in your area that carries your dream car.
- Most of the major auto manufacturers have Web sites where you can "build" a customized version of your dream car online.
- Key search words: dream car, dream car rentals

The little unremembered acts
of kindness and love
are the best parts of a person's life.

WILLIAM WORDSWORTH

number

10

Random Acts of Kindness

Who knew a selfless day of benevolent giving could be so compelling? Ask those who have tried it, and they will assure you it's something they want to do again and again. It really is true that when you're good to others, you're good to yourself. That translates easily to a truly satisfying date.

Tell your sweetheart ahead of time what you have in mind, and begin looking for places to invest your acts of kindness. If you're paying attention, opportunities won't be difficult to find. Do you have an elderly neighbor who could use some help with her lawn? Or do you know someone who needs help painting his house? Check out your local chapter of Habitat for Humanity. Call your town's homeless shelter and find out how you can be of service. Ask a nursing home if you can visit the residents. Many of them may enjoy being read to or would like to have a letter written for them.

Need is not in short supply in our country, but it sometimes is pushed to the side. Such a date will give you both a better understanding of what really matters in life — and also a better understanding of each other.

BUDGET

$ Guaranteed — this one won't cost you a dime!

STEPS TO SUCCESS

- Don't just show up at the nursing home or shelter. Call ahead.
- Wear comfortable clothes and shoes.
- Leave your money and valuables at home.
- Put a smile on your face and keep it there no matter what you see or hear.
- Remember that this date is not about you.

OVER THE TOP

- Contact the Red Cross for information on natural disaster training. Together you can make a difference when people need help the most.

GET CONNECTED

- Check out **volunteermatch.org** and **redcross.org**.
- If you are a nature lover, many zoos, state parks, and animal shelters need volunteers.
- Key search words: volunteer opportunities followed by your city and state

number

11

Window-Shopping

If you're looking for something to do but don't want to spend a lot of money, visit your local mall or an upscale shopping area and do some window-shopping. Check out the latest electronic gadgets. Get ideas for decorating your home. Visit the toy store, and have fun playing with the display items. Take some goofy photos together in a photo booth. Treat yourselves to lunch at a restaurant you've never tried before. And be sure to keep your eyes and ears open; after all, this is the perfect opportunity to get gift ideas for your sweetheart for future occasions.

BUDGET

$–$$ Window-shopping doesn't cost a thing, but you will want to plan to spend a little for lunch and anything you might find to do along the way. You could also plan a small amount to spend on a just-for-fun purchase.

STEPS TO SUCCESS

- Remember that the reason you're there is to have fun together, so avoid the temptation to "bargain shop" unless it's for something you're both excited about.

- Try to divide your time equally between things he's interested in and things she wants to look at. If you stop in a clothing store for her, make your next stop a music store or something else of his choice.

OVER THE TOP

- Visit the Mall of America in Minnesota. In addition to over 500 stores, it houses an amusement park, an aquarium, a fourteen-screen movie theater, and many other attractions.

GET CONNECTED

- For information about the Mall of America, visit **mallofamerica.com.**

- Key search words: shopping, shopping malls followed by your city and state

Romance Him

Whether or not he enjoys poetry, a poem written
by you telling of your love for him is a beautiful gift.
Then have it framed as a keepsake of your
abiding love. The poem does not have to be perfect
in rhyme or meter. What he will cherish is the
memory of the time, thought, and love
that went into the writing of the poem.

Play Laser Tag or Paintball

This is a great idea for a date and even more fun if you ask other couples to join you. Either way, the competition, the intrigue, and the sneaking about all add up to a top-notch event.

Laser tag is completely benign and appropriate for all ages. Paintball, on the other hand, is not for wimps. The paintball pellets actually sting, and it's messy. Experienced paintball players will tell you though — it's much more exciting than laser tag. Often played outdoors, there are many more opportunities for strategy and role-playing. Both laser tag and paintball offer an opportunity to rescue and defend each other or deliver romantic "you are my hero" kisses between rounds.

BUDGET

$$ Laser tag prices are reasonable. Paintball prices may be higher if you have to pay extra for supplies.

WHAT TO TAKE

For paintball:

- Good shoes for running
- Mask
- Some type of head protection
- Cloth for cleaning your mask
- Bottled water
- Bug spray

OVER THE TOP

- Rent the paintball facility for your group exclusively. Afterward, arrange to have a picnic on the property with all the fixings. Even if they don't provide food, they will probably allow you to bring your own.

GET CONNECTED

- Key search words: paintball, laser tag with your city and state, paintball or laser tag equipment

number

13

Say Cheese!

If you're not married or you've been married for a while or especially if you have kids, it's probably been awhile since you've had a picture taken of just the two of you. Why not have a portrait made? You could dress nicely and go with a traditional pose, or you could do something off the wall — something that demonstrates your individual personalities. If you're into sports, you could wear your fan gear. Or you could wear period clothing from an era you've always been intrigued by. Wear crazy hats or include something more subtle in the picture, like a small finger puppet peeking out of one of your pockets. Have fun and be creative, and allow your photographer creative license as well.

Another fun variation of this idea is to have your caricature drawn. You may be able to find a caricaturist doing drawings at your local mall, an amusement park, or in an entertainment district of town on weekends. Whether you decide on a portrait or caricature, you'll have a fun memento to enjoy for years to come.

BUDGET

$–$$ Cost will depend upon what studio you go to and how many pictures you purchase. Be sure to check the studio's Web site before you go for current special offers. Caricatures are usually fairly inexpensive.

OVER THE TOP

- Take an art class together, and attempt drawing portraits of each other.
- Have an artist draw, paint, or sculpt a portrait of the two of you. If you really want to go "over the top," have this done on the streets of New Orleans, New York, or even Paris.

GET CONNECTED

- Key search words: portraits, caricatures, caricaturists followed by your city and state

Night Golf

Who plays golf at night? It's so dark you can't tell your woods from your drivers! Okay, so nine holes are out of the question, but you should be able to see well enough to do some putting on the green closest to the clubhouse. You'll do even better if you purchase a glow-in-the-dark golf ball. Yes, there really is such a thing.

This date is more about being together than improving your golf swing, but it really can be great fun. If all the courses in your area are posted with signs which say "Keep Out After Dark" or are locked up tight, try a driving range. Those are almost always open at night, and you can have a great time with a basket or two of balls and a couple of drivers — all of which you can get right there at the range.

BUDGET

$ Night golf on an unrestricted, community course is literally free. Invest in a couple of those fancy glow-in-the-dark balls, borrow a couple of putters, and you're in business. A large basket of balls at the driving range is fairly inexpensive.

WHAT TO TAKE

- Light jacket
- Flashlight
- Golf balls and putters

STEPS TO SUCCESS

- Many driving ranges stay booked up and require reservations as much as a week in advance.
- Wear golf shoes or tennis shoes.

- Some golf courses would have no problem with your being there at night as long as you don't do any damage. However, it's best to call during business hours and ask if what you wish to do is permitted.
- Leave greens the way you found them.

GET CONNECTED

- Key search words: glow golf balls, golf course followed by your town and state

Put your hand on a hot stove
for a minute and it seems like an hour,
sit next to a pretty woman for an hour
and it seems like a minute.
That's relativity.

ALBERT EINSTEIN

number

15

Alphabet Date

Simple and entertaining, this makes a great date. Choose a letter — any letter. Putting all the letters in a hat and drawing one out is a great way to decide. Then agree that everything you do on your date will begin with that letter. For example, if your letter is "m," you will want to go to a movie or museum. If your letter is "w," you might go window-shopping or waterskiing. Carry this theme throughout the night with every place you go and everything you do. It will soon become a challenge, but one that you will have a great time figuring out together.

Make the suggestion for this date before the big night. That way no one will have made plans that have to be scrapped.

BUDGET

$ Depends on what letter you choose and what you want to make of it.

STEPS TO SUCCESS

- Take along a pocket dictionary — you'll need it.

- Dress for any eventuality you may encounter.

- Set your ground rules before you start. How completely do you want to go forward with this adventure? How far away are you willing to go?

- After choosing your letter, take a moment to brainstorm places and activities so you don't stand around for hours looking blankly into each other's eyes.

OVER THE TOP

- Invite other couples to go along with you. Let each couple choose a letter. Set a meeting place and a time. The couple that does the most things or finds the most places that correspond to their letter wins. For verification, have them snap a picture on their cell phone or camera at each stop.

Antique Car Show

Cars and cars and more cars — all wearing a polished shine you can see your face in. Beautiful, bright red classics. Adorable little sports coupes. Cars with fins. Cars with pinstripes. Cars with colorful flames lapping at their sides. Music, lights, and more excitement than you know what to do with! What a great place to stage a date! No matter what age group you and your date fall into, this should be a satisfying event. Most medium to large cities will have at least one show a year. Next time you feel like doing something different, see what your special someone has to say about exploring the health and well-being of the auto industry.

BUDGET

$–$$ Car show ticket prices vary widely, so call ahead or check for the price online. Plan a few extra dollars for parking as well.

WHAT TO TAKE

- Comfortable shoes
- Sunglasses, sunscreen, and a hat if the show is outside
- Camera — so you can take pictures of your date in front of some really classy numbers.

GET CONNECTED

- Key search words: antique car shows followed by your city and state

Indoor Rock Climbing

This may seem like an extreme date, but it really isn't. Even children can manage this sport with proper instruction. You will both need to be in good physical condition, however.

Spend some time together preparing for this exciting event studying technique online. By the time you arrive, you will both be completely hyped and ready to take on your challenge. Climb side by side or one behind the other so you can encourage and cheer each other on. On your way home, stop someplace where you can spend some time discussing how truly strong, brave, and amazing you both are while sipping a nutrition-conscious fruit smoothie or a hot cup of green tea.

BUDGET

$$ Prices vary from gym to gym. Be sure to ask if equipment rental and training is included.

WHAT TO TAKE

- Comfortable, loose-fitting clothing that allows you a full range of motion, such as T-shirts, shorts, sweatpants, or leggings
- A sweatshirt to keep you warm when you aren't climbing
- Shoes should have rubber soles with a good grip and fit as tightly as possible on your feet.

OVER THE TOP

- Rent a mobile rock-climbing wall and have a party in the backyard! Invite other couples and have some fun. After working up an appetite, fire up the grill.

GET CONNECTED

- At **indoorclimbing.com** you can locate a facility in your area. A climbing simulator is also available to help you enhance your skills. You can find out how to tailor your physical fitness program in preparation for rock-climbing training. And you can find out what equipment is required and where you can purchase or rent it.

- Key search words: rent a rock-climbing wall followed by your city and state

How Do I Love Thee?

How do I love thee? Let me count the ways.
I love thee to the depth and breadth and height
My soul can reach, when feeling out of sight
For the ends of Being and ideal Grace.
I love thee to the level of every day's
Most quiet need, by sun and candle-light.

ELIZABETH BARRETT BROWNING

Tour a Local Factory

Imagine yourself in Willy Wonka's chocolate factory taking a dip in a chocolate river or having your taste buds tantalized by a melt-in-your-mouth treat. Maybe you can't do that, but you can see real-life places where your favorite treats are made. Many factories have opened their doors to the public. Some have gift stores and, most exciting, some even offer free samples. Whatever your fancy, whether it be edible treats or pottery or toys, most areas in the country boast a factory or two. Many provide guest tours which can be both entertaining and educational. Some even offer exciting interactive exhibits such as the Boeing jet plant in the state of Washington.

Make a list of your favorite things, and see what you can find in your area that would make you both shiver with anticipation.

BUDGET

$ Typically, companies do not charge for a tour of their facilities. They are proud to show you around. Exceptions are companies that are espionage sensitive, such as fashion and technology producers.

STEPS TO SUCCESS

- Wear comfortable shoes and a light sweater or jacket you can take off. Some plants are very warm, others icy.
- Leave what you don't need in the car. You'll want your hands free to grab free samples.
- Many companies will not allow you to take photos. Be sure to ask.

GET CONNECTED

- Key search words: factories, factory tours followed by your city and state

number
19

Shall We Dance?

Has it been awhile since you stepped foot on a dance floor? If so, maybe it's time to dust off your dancing shoes and take a whirl around the floor with your sweetheart. What kind of dancing do you enjoy? There are many styles to choose from — ballroom, line dancing, the two-step, swing, salsa — the list goes on and on. If you're new to dance, watch an instructional DVD or take lessons before you go out on your own. Even if you can hold your own on the dance floor, try a new style you've never attempted before. You'll have fun learning something new together, and dancing is a great way to stay in shape as well. If you have trouble finding a place to show off your new moves, check with local dance studios that teach couples' classes. Many of them host open dances or will have some suggestions on where to go dancing.

BUDGET

$–$$$ Prices will vary depending on whether you choose to take lessons or purchase a DVD and teach yourselves.

OVER THE TOP

- Create your own private dance floor on a patio or in a room with wood or tile floors. Decorate with items such as flowers, candles, tulle, and white Christmas lights. Prepare a CD ahead of time with a mix of your favorite romantic songs that will fit the dance styles you've been practicing. Get dressed up for the occasion as if you were going out. If you wish, start your evening with a white tablecloth, candlelight dinner, and then dance the night away.

GET CONNECTED

- Key search words: ballroom dancing, country dancing, salsa dancing, swing dance, dance DVDs, dance instruction

Romance is the glamour
which turns the dust of everyday life
into a golden haze.

ELINOR GLYN

Drive-In Movie Theater

A fun alternative to the traditional dinner-and-a-movie date is the drive-in theater. While perhaps not as popular as in their glory days, drive-ins have been making a comeback in the last few years, and at least one of these hidden treasures can be found in most cities. They boast huge screens, and many have updated sound systems that broadcast over your radio. Some drive-ins will show two or even three movies for one admission, so you can stay for as many as you'd like. A night spent under the stars at the drive-in is so much more than just watching a movie — it's a fun, nostalgic, romantic experience you'll not soon forget.

BUDGET

$$ Most drive-in admissions are comparable to or less than a regular theater, but remember to take some extra cash for the snack bar.

WHAT TO TAKE

- You can pack your own snacks and drinks or plan on visiting the snack bar. If you're planning on staying for more than one feature, you may even want to take along something for dinner that can be eaten easily in the car.

- Include blankets and pillows so you can get comfortable, especially if it's chilly out.

OVER THE TOP

- Get online and find some drive-ins that sound especially fun or historically significant. Then get some other couples on board and plan a fun road trip to visit these theaters. You can keep the cost down by sharing hotel rooms. Find interesting, historic places to eat and sleep along the way.

GET CONNECTED

- Check out **driveinmovie.com** or **driveintheater.com** for up-to-date listings and descriptions of operating drive-ins in each state.

- Key search words: drive-in movie followed by your city and state

Love spends his all,
and still hath store.

P. J. BAILEY

number
21

Go Fishing

Fishing is a lot more than sitting on the bank with a cane pole — though that could be a lovely date as well. It's an exciting sport and one that would make for a genuinely entertaining day. Just imagine yourself catching the "big one"!

If you don't have the equipment to go fishing, it's easy to find at your local sporting goods store. Go together, since choosing lures is a very personal activity. If you want live bait, you can usually find it at a bait store located conveniently near the lake.

Rent a boat or just cast from the shore. It won't take more than a few minutes to get the hang of it. Chat away or simply be quiet together. Feel the sun on your face and the breeze in your hair. Focus on each cast, and then share the experience with each other over a picnic lunch. If you actually catch a fish — well, that's just icing on the cake.

BUDGET

$$ If you already have equipment or can borrow some, you'll be way ahead. You'll both need a fishing license, which can be purchased almost anywhere — hardware stores, bait and tackle shops, any store that has a fishing department.

WHAT TO TAKE

- Fishing rods and tackle
- Bottled water
- Lunch
- Hat
- Sunscreen
- Wet wipes
- Jacket
- Comfortable shoes with rubber soles
- Net and bucket

OVER THE TOP

- Hire a fishing guide, and see how many you can catch!
  The winner must buy lunch at a fancy seafood restaurant.

GET CONNECTED

- Be sure to ask the locals where the best fishing is.
- Key search words: fishing, fishing lures, fishing guides

Keep love in your heart.
A life without it is like
a sunless garden
when the flowers are dead.

OSCAR WILDE

number

22

Carriage Ride

Step back in time and enjoy the charm and romance of a horse-drawn carriage ride. These rides are often offered in downtown areas or in historic districts. They can be arranged ahead of time or are usually available as a spur-of-the-moment idea, perhaps as the crowning jewel to a nice dinner out. The drivers will many times have interesting tidbits to share about the surrounding area along the way. Snuggle up, enjoy the scenery, and imagine yourselves in a different time.

BUDGET

$$ Prices will vary depending on location, but most horse-drawn carriage rides are reasonable for something to do that is out of the ordinary.

OVER THE TOP

- If you live in an area that gets heavy snowfalls, an old-fashioned horse-drawn sleigh ride is a romantic wintertime diversion.
- For a more adventurous date, skip the carriage and get right on the horse! Horseback riding can be a fun experience, even for beginners. Some stables even offer special packages that include a campfire dinner or cattle-drive experience.
- Visit New York City, and take a carriage ride through Central Park.

GET CONNECTED

- Key search words: horse-drawn carriage rides, horse-drawn sleigh rides, horseback riding

number

23

Get Literary

Explore your intellectual side. Even if you're not an avid reader, you might be surprised at the conversations a visit to a bookstore, library, or book fair can spark. Browse the shelves, and talk about anything that draws your attention. If you're not in the habit of reading, find a book about something that interests you — a sport or hobby or something you've wanted to learn more about. It might be fun to visit the children's section and both try to find your favorite childhood bedtime story.

If you are in the market for a good read or just enjoy the thrill of the hunt, a used-book store or book fair is a great choice. From early editions of literary classics to collectors' editions of your favorite comic books, you're sure to find something that interests you, and often at surprisingly reasonable prices.

BUDGET

$ Browsing a library or bookstore is free, but take along a little money in case you decide to visit the coffee bar. Libraries also have regular used-book sales that might offer something of interest.

OVER THE TOP

• Form a private book club for two. Choose a book. (You may want to purchase or check out a copy for each of you.) Read it separately; then talk about it over dessert at a coffee shop or café. If one of you isn't a reader, get the book on tape from your local library.

GET CONNECTED

• Key search words: bookstore, library, book club books

Romance Her

Treat her to a fancy dinner under the stars.
You will need a card table, two chairs, a white
tablecloth and napkins, china plates, goblets,
silverware, a vase of flowers, candles in candlesticks,
and the best take-out food you can afford.
Take care to research your location.
She'll be dazzled!

Engage in a Friendly Competition

Who's the most competitive? Do either of you have any hidden talents the other doesn't know about? A little friendly competition can provide a fun way to spend time together, and you just may discover something new about each other along the way. Pick something that you both enjoy doing or maybe something you've never or only rarely tried before. You could go bowling, play pool or miniature golf, or take a swing at the batting cages.

You may even want to make it more interesting by agreeing on a prize for the winner — such as the loser treats the winner to dessert or the winner gets to pick the next movie you see together. Or purchase a trophy or other small memento of your evening to go to the winner. You could even agree to pass it back and forth to the winner on future dates.

BUDGET

$ Most of these activities are relatively inexpensive and can provide hours of fun.

STEPS TO SUCCESS

- If you tend to be very competitive, make sure you keep it lighthearted and don't get so caught up in the game that you forget your main goal of having fun together.
- Have fun laughing with each other, but make sure it's all in good fun (for both of you) and that you steer clear of anything that could be hurtful.
- Cheer each other on, and celebrate one another's successes.

OVER THE TOP

- Join a local team or league together and make it a regular event.

GET CONNECTED

- Key search words: miniature golf, bowling, billiards, trophies

Life is a flower
of which love
is the honey.

VICTOR HUGO

number
25

Trash or Treasure?

You've probably heard the old adage, "One man's trash is another man's treasure." Why not see if this idea rings true for the two of you? Visit some yard sales or estate sales, or go to a flea market, thrift store, or antique shop together. Have fun finding unusual items or things that bring back special memories for you. While you're there, have a contest to see who can find the ugliest or most unusual item. You may even want to purchase your finds as a gift for each other and a fun memento of your date.

BUDGET

$–$$ This date should be fairly inexpensive — unless, of course, you find lots of "treasures" you just can't leave behind.

OVER THE TOP

- Look for an item you think may be priced well below its value, then try selling it online. If you make a profit, celebrate over dinner at a fancy restaurant or some other activity you normally wouldn't treat yourselves to.

- Look up some unusual items online, or think of your favorite childhood toys that aren't around anymore. Make a list beforehand, and then go on a scavenger hunt to see how many of these items you can find at sales or stores in your area.

GET CONNECTED

- Many newspapers have online listings of yard sales in the area. Type in the name of the paper, then look under the "classifieds" section.

- Key search words: antiques, thrift store, flea market, yard sale, garage sale

To love is to find pleasure
in the happiness
of the person loved.

LEIBNITZ

Visit a Botanical Garden or Garden Show

There's something romantic about being surrounded by beautiful flowers, trees, and ornamental plants. Enjoy walking hand in hand and admiring the wonders of nature artistically displayed at a botanical garden. While this activity is a great choice for a nice, sunny day, many gardens also feature large greenhouse areas that can be enjoyed year-round.

Another fun option is to attend a garden show. Some shows include a variety of plants, while others feature a certain type of plant, such as roses or bonsai trees. And many include demonstrations and classes so you can learn more about planting and growing these items yourself. You may even wish to purchase a plant for your sweetheart and enjoy planting and taking care of it together.

BUDGET

$–$$ There is usually a modest entry fee for botanical gardens or garden shows. Take extra money in case you want to make a purchase.

WHAT TO TAKE

- Take along a picnic to enjoy on the grounds. (Call beforehand to make sure picnicking is permitted.)

OVER THE TOP

- Invite another couple or two on a road trip to visit several gardens. Choose a major garden, such as the New York Botanical Gardens, as your final destination.
- Grow a bonsai tree together. For information, check out **bonsaigardener.com.**

GET CONNECTED

- **Wikipedia.com** provides a comprehensive list of botanical gardens in each state. Go to the Web site and type in "list of botanical gardens in the United States."
- Key search words: botanical gardens, garden show, rose show, bonsai show

Real love —
the lasting kind —
benefits others at the
expense of oneself.

ANONYMOUS

number

27

Take a Hike!

Instead of telling each other to "take a hike," take one together. Plan a day trip to a state or national park and explore the hiking trails. You might want to stop at the park office or visitor center on your way in and pick up a map. Choose a trail that fits your level of fitness and experience and head out for an adventure. Keep your ears tuned in and your eyes open for interesting birds and other wildlife; take time to notice details along the way, such as pretty wildflowers, ferns, moss, and insects.

BUDGET

$ Some parks charge a small day-use fee, but many allow you to explore free of charge.

WHAT TO TAKE

- A backpack, layered clothing, and comfortable shoes
- Plenty of bottled water
- Trail mix and/or energy bars
- Binoculars
- A compass
- If there are any caves you want to explore along the trail, you'll need a flashlight. Check your map to make sure the cave isn't off-limits to visitors.
- A small first-aid kit
- Cell phone or GPS device

OVER THE TOP

- For the really adventurous (experienced hikers only, please!), some parks offer heli-hiking expeditions in which you're flown by helicopter to a certain destination. You then hike your way back to a pickup spot. You'll need to make sure you're physically ready and have the right gear for this adventure.

- Take a rock-climbing course together. Then plan some day trips to try out your skills.

GET CONNECTED

- Go to **nps.gov** to find a complete listing of national parks. State parks can be found by searching for the name of the state followed by the words state parks.
- Key search words: hiking, hiking trails, bird watching

First Love

I ne'er was struck before that hour
With love so sudden and so sweet,
Her face it bloomed like a sweet flower
And stole my heart away complete.

I never saw so sweet a face
As that I stood before
My heart has left its dwelling place
And can return no more.

JON CLARE

number 28

Go Horseback Riding!

Whether you're an expert equestrian or your last and only horseback-riding experience was the pony ride at the state fair, an afternoon at the riding stables can be an exciting, romantic adventure. If you're new to horseback riding, most riding stables will give you a short prep course about how to handle the horses and provide guided expeditions if you're uncomfortable going out on your own. They also try to match the horse's temperament with your level of experience. So saddle up and hit the trail for a great new adventure with the one you love.

BUDGET

$$ Fees will vary from stable to stable and may depend partly on how scenic the trail is. Make sure the stable you choose stresses safety and offers a good introductory course.

WHAT TO TAKE

- Comfortable clothing that covers your arms and legs
- Heavy shoes or boots
- A hat and a jacket
- Insect repellent

OVER THE TOP

- Go on a special "themed" expedition. Some stables offer rides that include a campfire meal and/or entertainment. Others will let you get a taste of what it would be like to work on a ranch rounding up cattle.
- If you're near the ocean, go horseback riding on the beach.
- If you can time your ride around sunrise or sunset, it's a special treat!

GET CONNECTED

- Key search words: horseback riding, riding stables, horseback riding on the beach, horseback ride with meal

And what is a kiss, when all is done?
A promise given under seal — a vow
A signature acknowledged — a rosy dot
Over the I of Loving — a secret whispered
To listening lips apart — a moment made
Immortal, with a rush of wings unseen —
A sacrament of blossoms, a new song
Sung by two hearts to an old simple tune —
The ring of one horizon around two souls
Together, all alone!

EDMOND ROSTAND

Have a Zoolightful Date

You may think of the zoo as a place for kids, but it can provide a fun day of entertainment for anyone. Many zoos allow visitors to feed certain animals in interactive exhibits, and most zoos have live animal demonstrations or shows daily. In addition to the animals, which provide new and different entertainment every time you visit, many zoos also host some beautiful landscaping and gardens, making them great places to walk and talk while getting some fresh air.

There are also many wildlife sanctuaries which are usually privately owned and funded. These refuges take in abused and neglected animals. They usually don't have fancy facilities but can sometimes offer a more "up close and personal" experience with the animals than you would find at a zoo.

Go ahead — take a walk on the wild side with the stars of the animal kingdom.

BUDGET

$–$$ Most zoos have reasonable admission prices. Take a little extra for the snack bar, train rides, and souvenirs.

WHAT TO TAKE

- Most zoos will allow you to take along a picnic, or you can plan to eat at the snack bar.
- Sunglasses and sunscreen
- Binoculars to help you see animals you might otherwise miss
- Comfortable shoes and clothes
- Camera

OVER THE TOP

- Have fun trying to identify which type of animal each of you most resembles based on appearance, personality traits, etc. Take pictures of each other with the chosen animals. Choose carefully; you could get yourself into trouble!

- Some zoos host special benefit dinners, dances, or concerts on their grounds. Make plans to attend one of these special events.
- Take a behind-the-scenes tour with a zookeeper. These can be expensive and need to be booked well in advance.

GET CONNECTED

- On **aza.com,** you can find a zoo in your area that is accredited by the Association of Zoos and Aquariums. In order to be accredited, a zoo must meet high standards of commitment to conservation, ensure humane treatment of animals, and provide habitats that mimic the animals' natural environments as closely as possible.
- Key search words: wildlife refuge or wildlife sanctuary followed by your city and state

number

30

Hit the Deck

For a marine adventure you'll always remember, rent a sailboat, pontoon boat, or paddleboat, and head out on the lake for a day of fun in the sun. If there are several marinas on the lake, you could plan to dock and explore other areas along the way. Or if you live near one, take a ferry ride and explore the sights when you reach your destination. Keep an eye out for the birds, fish, turtles, and other wildlife along the way. You never know what new sights you may see.

BUDGET

$–$$$ The amount you spend will vary greatly depending on which activity you choose. If budget is a concern, a paddleboat may be the vessel of choice.

WHAT TO TAKE

- Be sure to take sunscreen and sunglasses.

- Wear comfortable shoes that don't get slick when wet.

- You may want a light jacket since temperatures tend to be lower and winds stronger over water.

- If you'll be out for a while, take a picnic lunch or some snacks and drinks.

OVER THE TOP

- Make arrangements to arrive a little early and deck the boat out with flowers and other simple decorations. Hide a small token of your affection or love notes somewhere onboard for your sweetheart to discover along the way.

- If you live near the coast, take a day cruise. Although the boats used are smaller than the big cruise liners, they still offer many of the amenities, including swimming pools, restaurants, and shows.

GET CONNECTED

- Many state parks offer boat rentals and provide information on their Web sites.
- Key search words: boat rentals, sailboat rentals, paddleboats, ferry rides, day cruises

Love is a canvas
furnished by nature
and embroidered
by imagination.

VOLTAIRE

Some people
come into our lives
and quickly go.
Some stay for a while
and leave footprints on our hearts.
And we are never, ever the same.

ANONYMOUS

number
31

Go to the Fair

A county or state fair can provide something out of the ordinary to do on a date. Besides the rides and carnival games, most fairs also offer free concerts and other entertainment. You could explore your love of animals in the livestock arena and petting barn or take a look at some local artwork. See the latest and greatest in automobiles and gadgets. Of course, you can't go to the fair without sampling some fair food. Have some of your old favorites — corn dogs, turkey legs, cotton candy, funnel cakes — or try something new, like fried mashed potatoes on a stick, apple fries, or chocolate-covered cheesecake. You could even speculate about what next year's new fried food on a stick might be!

BUDGET

$–$$ The cost of rides, games, and food at the fair can add up quickly, so if budget is a concern, take advantage of the free events and exhibits that are included in your admission.

OVER THE TOP

- Plan several months in advance to grow or make something together and enter it in the fair. Categories range from amateur photography to robotics, from baking to vegetable gardening. You should be able to find details about categories as well as entry rules and deadlines on the fair's Web site.

GET CONNECTED

- Most fairs will have a Web site where you can find pertinent information.
- Key search words: the name of your county or state followed by county/state fair

He Flies Through the Air with the Greatest of Ease

Who is he? The daring young man on the flying trapeze, of course! When is the last time you went to the circus? Find out when the next one is coming your way, and grab your sweetheart for an evening of three-ring excitement. Take a little trip down memory lane as you watch the circus stars perform daring acts and unbelievable stunts. Enjoy the funny antics of the clowns. And don't forget to enjoy some old favorites while you're there, like peanuts, popcorn, and cotton candy.

BUDGET

$$ Ticket prices vary according to location in the arena. Take along a little extra for snacks and perhaps a souvenir.

OVER THE TOP

- Some circuses offer special VIP tickets, which entitle the holder to prime seating as well as a moment in the spotlight participating in the performance. They also sometimes offer a preshow for those arriving early, during which you can meet the performers and enjoy some behind-the-scenes activities.

GET CONNECTED

- Key search words: circus, animal-free circuses

The giving of love
is an education
in itself.

ELEANOR ROOSEVELT

Love without friendship
is like a house
without a foundation.

DAVID VALENTINE

number
33

Fun at the Beach

If you live near the coast, the beach is the perfect place to spend a day with the one you love. Have a picnic on the beach. Wade along the shore, walking hand in hand. Build a sand castle together. Watch the sun set over the ocean, observing all the beautiful changes in color.

If you're landlocked, this date may take a little more creativity and imagination, but it can still be lots of fun. Take a picnic to a park that has a large sandbox area. Kick off your shoes and play tag in the sand. Build a sand castle. You could even take a couple of seashells with you, relax on your picnic blanket, and "listen to the ocean" by playing a CD of ocean sounds or by placing the seashell up to your ear. Close your eyes and imagine your dream vacation at the beach. Describe what you see to each other.

BUDGET

$ This is an inexpensive date that can provide hours of entertainment.

WHAT TO TAKE

- A picnic and picnic blanket
- Sunglasses and sunscreen
- Binoculars to look for aquatic life at the beach
- Comfortable shoes that you don't mind getting sandy
- A light jacket

OVER THE TOP

- If you're nowhere near a beach, plan a trip to one. Maybe one of you has relatives who live near the coast and would enjoy your visit.
- If you live near the beach and go often, try something you normally don't do. Visit the boardwalk or an old coastal town as if you were a tourist.

GET CONNECTED

- National seashores provide beautiful stretches of natural beaches to explore. Since they are protected, they aren't overdeveloped with hotels and resorts. You can find a list of them by going to **nps.gov** and doing a search for national seashores.

- If you're looking for a local park with sand, try a search for the name of your city followed by the word parks.

- Key search words: beach, seashore, boardwalk, seashells

A friend
is one who knows you
and loves you just the same.

ELBERT HUBBARD

Game Night

For a fun and relaxing night in, don some comfy clothes, pull out some snack foods, and challenge each other at your favorite board or card games. Who will be the first to arrive at millionaire acres? Which one of you will be the first to put the clues together to find out who did it, with what, and where? Is there a "card shark" in the house? Can you keep your right hand on the red dot, your left foot on the green dot, and your right foot on the yellow dot while reaching over your sweetheart to touch the blue dot with your left hand? Pick several shorter games, or immerse yourself in a longer game you both enjoy.

BUDGET

$ Unless you decide to buy a new game or stock up on snack foods, this date won't cost a dime!

OVER THE TOP

- Have a trophy made for the winner, or buy some other prize for the champion of the night.
- Go to the store and pick out a new game you've never tried before.

GET CONNECTED

- For game ideas, visit **Hasbro.com, mattel.com,** or **cranium.com.**
- Key search words: board games, card games

number
35

We All Scream for Ice Cream

Nothing beats a bowl of rich, creamy homemade ice cream on a hot summer day. And there's no better way to work up an appetite and have a great time in the process than to churn it yourself. Purchase or borrow an old-fashioned, hand-cranked ice-cream maker; then head to the grocery store to get the ingredients and your favorite toppings. Don't forget the ice and rock salt. Mix up your confectionary treat together, and then take turns churning it into a frozen delight. Finally, make your own sundaes, kick back, and enjoy the fruit of your labor.

BUDGET

$ This date is fairly inexpensive, especially if you already have or can borrow an ice-cream maker.

OVER THE TOP

- Before the date, decorate your dining room like an old-fashioned ice-cream parlor, complete with soda glasses, a fun tablecloth, straws in an antique-looking straw holder, and so forth. Play a CD of oldies in the background.

GET CONNECTED

- Key search words: homemade ice-cream recipes, sundae toppings

Romance Her

Leave an index card where she will find it,
and instruct her to follow the clues
for a pleasant surprise. On the back of the card,
give her the first clue that sends her
to the location of the next clue, and the next,
and the next, until she finds her way
to where you are waiting
with a kiss and flowers
or a small gift.

number 36

Take a Float Trip

Fasten your life vest, and plunge into a watery adventure. Find a river nearby that is good for floating, and rent a canoe, raft, or kayak for the day. If you're new to floating, make sure the river you choose is beginner friendly and that the establishment you rent your vessel from emphasizes safety. Most rental stores will also offer a ride back to your car when you're finished. Spend the day exploring, enjoying the water, and taking in the fresh air of the great outdoors.

BUDGET

$$ It's a good idea to check and compare rental rates.

WHAT TO TAKE

- Sunglasses (preferably with straps) and sunscreen
- Insect repellent
- A small first-aid kit
- Plenty of bottled water
- Life vests
- Shoes that fasten tightly on your feet
- Snacks or a picnic lunch
- A waterproof disposable camera
- A watertight container that floats to protect your supplies if your vessel should capsize

OVER THE TOP

- Take a kayaking or white-water rafting safety course together, and then head out for a thrilling adventure. Or go on a guided white-water rafting adventure designed for beginners.
- Purchase your own canoe, kayaks, or raft so you can go floating often.

GET CONNECTED

- Go to **raftingamerica.com** for great information on kayaking and white-water rafting.
- Go to **nps.gov** or the state park site for your state to find a listing of state and national parks in your area that offer canoe, raft, and/or kayak rentals.
- Key search words: canoeing, kayaking, rafting, white-water rafting

Let no one who loves
be called unhappy.
Even love unreturned
has its rainbow.

J. M. BARRIE

Go to a Theme Park

What could be more fun and thrilling than zooming into the air and then plummeting down at breakneck speeds on your favorite roller coaster? Spin, loop, fly, and bounce your way to a great date at a nearby theme park. After you've ridden a few rides, take a break and enjoy some of the in-park entertainment.

Talk about which rides were your favorites when you were a child, and enjoy some snacks while discussing it. While you're there, dare each other to try a ride you've never been on before — one that maybe you've been a little afraid of. If the park offers one, stick around after dark for the light show or fireworks display to top off your exciting day.

BUDGET

$$ Since there is a wide range of admission prices for theme parks, check rates before you make plans.

OVER THE TOP

- Visit one of these top-rated theme parks in the United States: Walt Disney World, Disneyland, Legoland, Busch Gardens, or Universal Studios.
- Try out one of these top-rated European parks: Port Aventura in Barcelona, Chessington or Thorpe Park in London.

GET CONNECTED

- To find theme parks in the United States listed by state, go to **themeparksonline.org.**
- Other good sights for theme park information are **themeparks.about.com** and **themeparkinsider.com.**
- Key search words: theme park followed by your city and state

number
38

Up, Up, and Away

Very few dates are as impressive as a ride in a hot-air balloon, flying high above the landscape, taking in a magnificent view, wind blowing through your hair. Can you imagine it? It is said to be one of the top ten things people want to experience in their lifetimes.

Because of the cost, you may have to save your pennies for a while, but the experience is breathtaking, unforgettable, and perfect for an ultra-special occasion. Some companies offer sweetheart packages, which are flights for two that include items like teddy bears, chocolates, champagne, and fresh flowers. Other packages include breakfast or lunch and lots of great extras. Though tough on the pocketbook, this date is guaranteed to wow just about anyone.

BUDGET

$$$ Hot-air balloon rides can be pricey, so this may be something you'll want to save for an extra-special occasion.

WHAT TO TAKE

- Comfortable, layered clothing
- Sturdy walking shoes (no high heels, please)
- Camera

STEPS TO SUCCESS

- Plan ahead. Almost all balloon rides must be booked no less than a week in advance.

GET CONNECTED

- Key search words: hot-air balloon ride, sweetheart packages for hot-air balloon ride

No cord nor cable
can so forcibly draw,
or hold so fast,
as love can do
with a twined thread.

ROBERT BURTON

number
39

Treasure Hunt

You may want to make this a group date if you are looking for over-the-top fun and excitement. But it can also be an exceptionally romantic date for two. Present your date with a handwritten clue that leads to another and another and another until the treasure is found. This is a clever way to present holiday gifts, birthday presents, or gifts of any kind, for that matter.

Make your clues romantic and provocative. Using a few lines of well-known love poetry is a good play. Alter a few words here and there to send your date searching in the right direction. Clues can be written on plain index cards or on elaborate creations with frills, bows, and lots of color. Happy hunting!

BUDGET

$ Depends completely on the cost of the treasure. Add a few dollars for materials for creating beautiful clue cards. Also include gas money if your hunt extends any distance from your starting place.

OVER THE TOP

- For the latest in treasure hunts, try geocaching. This is a game people play using GPS (global positioning system) devices in order to find caches left by others in different areas.

- A cache usually consists of a logbook which will have valuable information such as facts about the area, perhaps some jokes, and maybe even clues to the whereabouts of the next cache. It may also contain small items of interest.

- A GPS device will cost between $100 and $1000.

GET CONNECTED

- Check out **geocaching.com** for everything you need to know about geocaching.

- Key search words: treasure hunt, scavenger hunt, geocaching, GPS device

All that we love deeply
becomes a part of us.

HELEN KELLER

Fly a Kite

Sun, fun, and the great outdoors. Those are just a few of the reasons to stand next to your sweetie, bobbin of string in hand, and watch your kite float high above your heads. As it dips, weaves, and soars, you'll feel as if the two of you are doing the same. It's mesmerizing. Take turns holding the bobbin and feel free to experiment, seeing if you can make your kite go this way or that. Reel it in and let it back out. Run in the opposite direction and watch it follow — an absolute exercise in whimsy.

Take a picnic lunch with you to the park, and wile the day away making pretty circles in the sky. It's fun for one — and even more fun for two!

BUDGET

$–$$ You can spend quite a lot for a kite or next to nothing. The more expensive ones are often sturdier and more likely to be used again. But the simple, inexpensive variety will give you hours of fun for just a few dollars.

WHAT TO TAKE

- A kite
- Comfortable clothes and running shoes
- Sunscreen, sunglasses, and a hat
- Blanket and picnic basket
- Camera

STEPS TO SUCCESS

- Stay away from power lines.
- Don't try to fly kites in a storm or rainy weather (just ask Ben Franklin)!

- Choose an open field, meadow, or park where you can steer clear of trees.
- Use the string that comes with your kite or an approved type of kite line.

OVER THE TOP

- Enter a kite-flying competition.

GET CONNECTED

- Key search words: kite, kite flying, kite-flying competition

He is the half part of a blessed man
Left to be finished by such as she;
And she is fair divided excellence,
Whole fullness of perfection lies in him.
O, two such silver current, when they join,
Do glorify the banks that found them in!

GEOFFREY CHAUCER

Bicycle Built for Two

Have fun trying something new together and get a good workout at the same time. Find a bicycle shop that has rentals, and rent a tandem bicycle for the day. Take it for a leisurely ride along a scenic trail, or ride it around an area with shops and other points of interest where you could stop to take breaks along the way. You may wish to take a picnic lunch along with you, or you could stop at an outdoor café for lunch. Ask a passerby to take a picture of the two of you on the bike to commemorate the experience.

BUDGET

$$ Your main expense will be the bike rental. You may also need to purchase or rent helmets if you don't already own some.

WHAT TO TAKE

- Water bottles
- Sunscreen and sunglasses
- Bicycle helmets

OVER THE TOP

- Take a guided tandem bicycle tour of Ireland or some other location that offers these unique experiences.
- If you find this is something you really enjoy, consider purchasing your own tandem bicycle.
- Enter a tandem bike race and enjoy training together and working toward a goal together.

GET CONNECTED

- Key search words: tandem cycling, tandem tours, bike rentals

number

42

Romantic Movie Night

Turn an ordinary movie rental into a memorable private viewing event created just for the two of you. Set up a fancy candlelight dinner in view of the television so you can dine in style as you watch the movie. Or set up a luxurious seating area with plenty of pillows and blankets for snuggling, either on the floor or sofa. Add special touches with flowers and other decorations throughout the room. Get dressed up for the event as if you were attending an exclusive viewing party.

BUDGET

$–$$ Movie rentals are inexpensive. Other expenses may include dinner, flowers, and other decorations.

OVER THE TOP

- Some museums and community centers offer outdoor viewings of classic movies. See if you can find one of these special events in your area.
- Surprise your special someone by having a surround sound theater system installed just before your big movie night.
- Take a sleeping bag and portable DVD player to the backyard and watch your movie under the stars.

GET CONNECTED

- Key search words: movie rentals, romantic movies, movie on the lawn

Grow old along with me!
The best is yet to be.
The last of life, for which the first was made;
Our times are in his hand,
Who saith, "A whole I planned,
Youth shows but half; trust God:
See all, nor be afraid!"

ROBERT BROWNING

number
43

Become Art Critics

Tap into a plethora of great date activities by familiarizing yourself with your city's performing arts scene. Check your local newspaper or other local periodicals as well as your city's Web site for information about upcoming events. Attend a play or musical production put on by a community theater group. See if there is a Shakespeare in the Park organization in your area. Visit an area coffee shop on a night when they are hosting a live musical performance by a local artist. At Christmastime, attend a local production of Handel's *Messiah*, Dickens' *A Christmas Carol*, or Tchaikovsky's *The Nutcracker*. Check area churches and colleges for productions you might enjoy attending. While local performances may not always be as polished as a performance by a professional company, they are usually much more affordable, allowing you to attend more events, and you can feel good about supporting local artists and perhaps helping them to get their start.

BUDGET

$-$$ If you watch for them, you can probably find many events in your area that are free of charge.

WHAT TO TAKE

* Camera, just in case there is a photo opportunity with the cast
* Binoculars, if you don't have perfect seats

OVER THE TOP

* Purchase season passes to your local performing arts center or for a company or theater group you particularly enjoy.
* Join a community theater group and experience firsthand the thrill of performing.

GET CONNECTED

- Check the Web site of your city or your city's arts council for a calendar of events.
- Key search words: community theater, performing arts center, opera, ballet, local artists followed by your city and state

Love is love's reward.

JOHN DRYDEN

number
44

Extreme Adventure

Is there something extreme you've always wanted to try but haven't quite mustered up the courage to do yet? Combine your bravery and tackle it together. Go bungee jumping, skydiving, or hang gliding. Go on a heli-hike, an outdoor adventure in which you're taken to a drop-off spot by helicopter and must hike your way back to the pickup location. Take a white-water rafting trip. Whatever your extreme ambition might be, take it on together and create a memory you'll tell others about for years to come.

BUDGET

$$–$$$ Some of these adventures can be quite pricey, but keep in mind that it's a once-in-a-lifetime experience and a memory that will last forever.

OVER THE TOP

- Backpack your way through Europe, staying in hostels along the way.
- Go on an African safari or other extreme adventure tour.
- Dogfight in a real fighter plane or take a race car for a spin on a super speedway. NASCAR offers racing schools at selected speedways with instruction and actual driving time in a race car.

GET CONNECTED

- Key search words: bungee jumping, skydiving, hang gliding, heli-hike, white-water rafting, extreme adventures, fly in a fighter jet, drive a race car, rock climbing

number
45

Get Historical

For a fun and interesting outing that can be educational, too, visit a museum or other local historical landmark. Before you go, arm yourself with information from the Internet so you can make the most of your visit. Talk about items and facts that are particularly interesting to you and about how your perception of history may have differed from reality. Share how the history you're learning may relate to your family's history. You may want to check the museum's calendar of events and plan your visit around a special exhibit, event, or historical reenactment.

BUDGET

$ Some museums charge a nominal entry fee, while others rely on donations.

OVER THE TOP

- Take a road trip following a historic highway or pioneer trail. Make lots of stops along the way to explore the history of the area.
- Participate as actors in a historical reenactment.
- Visit the National Mall and Smithsonian in Washington, D.C., and immerse yourself in U.S. history.
- Many states also have whimsical landmarks. For example, Kansas boasts of having the nation's largest sunflower. Make it an ongoing goal to visit as many state landmarks as you can. Have a designated photo album for all your adventures.

GET CONNECTED

- For wacky landmarks, check out **roadsideamerica.com** or Google unusual landmarks followed by the state you are interested in.
- Key search words: national or historical landmarks, museums, historic highways, pioneer trails, or historical reenactment followed by specific state, Smithsonian

Croquet on the Lawn

Croquet, better know in England than in the U.S., is a sport known for its advanced gentility. Football and hockey devotees will find it remarkably docile. But some might argue that cutthroat competition and groveling in the dirt are not well suited to the civilities of dating.

Consider for a moment the bevy of benefits croquet can offer: (1) brisk exercise, (2) the challenge of conquering a sport played by kings and queens, (3) an opportunity to become familiar with mallets, and (4) one of the few sports you can actually engage in while carrying on a credible conversation. Not bad!

Set up your croquet set on the lawn, and make a date for a big play-off to be held on the next sunny afternoon. Up the stakes a bit by declaring that the loser buys the winner an ice-cream sundae.

BUDGET

$–$$ You probably already have a croquet set — no?
Then you will have to purchase one.

STEPS TO SUCCESS

- Sports equipment stores usually sell croquet sets.
- If you don't have a yard, set up at a local park.

OVER THE TOP

- Dress up for the big game. Women should wear a dress,
  loose fitting and of a light, airy fabric. Men should wear
  knickers, and bow ties are encouraged.

GET CONNECTED

- Key search words: new croquet set, used croquet set,
  history of croquet

Love is like swallowing
hot chocolate before it has cooled off.
It takes you by surprise at first,
but keeps you warm for a long time.

AUTHOR UNKNOWN

number
47

All Aboard!

Passenger trains aren't as easily accessible as they used to be, but if you have a historic, scenic railroad nearby, you have the makings of a charming and greatly enjoyable date. Short-run scenic trains usually provide opportunities to view splendid autumn colors, breathtaking landscapes, and snow scenes from observation cars with full-length windows and glass ceilings. Many include dinner. And some provide entertainment — singers, musicians, or even interactive role playing.

No doubt about it, an excursion train trip can be that special date you're looking for and one which will engender many fond memories.

BUDGET

$$–$$$ Costs for excursion trains vary widely, depending on the length of the trip and the extras offered.

STEPS TO SUCCESS

- Book early.
- Dress comfortably. Layers are best since temperatures inside the cars vary widely — some are cold and drafty, others warm and stuffy.
- Wear sunglasses. Glare in observation cars can be intense.
- Turn off your cell phone.
- For longer rides, take along something to read.
- Don't forget your camera.

OVER THE TOP

- Take a train trip vacation, enjoying all the scenery you might not see by car. Imagine snuggling together in your compartment as you watch the sun set outside your window.

GET CONNECTED

- You can find a directory of scenic railroads listed by state at **railusa.com.**
- Check out **amtrak.com** for vacation packages.
- Key search words: train vacation packages, dinner trains

Sing Your Hearts Out

A date for karaoke is not for the fainthearted. It's probable
that you will hear some truly disturbing performances of
some of your favorite songs. But that's part of the fun. Plus,
it leaves you thinking positively about your own rendition
of the Righteous Brothers' "Unchained Melody" or Queen's
"Bohemian Rhapsody" or — well ... you decide.

Karaoke can be found all over town these days. All you
have to do is take a number and your place in the audience.
Opt for beverages without ice to preserve your voice timbre.
(That's what the pros do.) When it's your turn, try a duet.
The words will be projected on a screen in front of you, so
no worries. Just sing your little hearts out — and then laugh
until you think you'll drop. Beware. Some couples have
had so much fun on this date that they have caught the
"entertainment bug," returning week after week for the
lights, the music, and the applause.

BUDGET

$$ You'll need to cover beverages and finger food or perhaps dinner. Some places have a cover charge.

OVER THE TOP

- Purchase a favorite CD and rehearse your performance at home.
- Buy karaoke equipment and have your own karaoke parties at home.

GET CONNECTED

- Key search words: karaoke followed by your city and state, karaoke machine

number
49

Day at the Spa

Imagine for a moment the two of you lying facedown on side-by-side massage tables, holding hands across the distance in between. Soothing music is playing. Oils are burning nearby, releasing exotic fragrances into the air, while massage therapists bring relief to stressed muscles and push the tension from your bodies. Now that's a date! And when the massages are over, spas have many other luxuries in which to indulge, like skin treatments for both men and women, healthy lunches, and much more.

You can book a full day or just a lazy afternoon. Whatever you choose, it will keep you thinking beautiful thoughts about each other for a long time to come.

BUDGET

$$$ Spa dates can be pricey, so you will want to save up for this one. Your best bet is to look for specials on sweetheart packages.

STEPS TO SUCCESS

- Book early to get the best package and the dates you prefer.
- Friday afternoons are ideal. You have the weekend to relax.
- Turn off your cell phones.

OVER THE TOP

- Book a full weekend and take advantage of all the spa has to offer.

GET CONNECTED

- Key search words: spa or spa packages followed by your city and state

How many times do I love again?
Tell me how many beads there are
In a silver chain of evening rain
Unravelled from the trembling main
And threading the eye of a yellow star —
So many times do I love again.

THOMAS LOVELL BEDDOES

number
50

Retro Date

You love to dress up, so why not make a night of it? You can choose any decade you like — poodle skirts and greasy hair for the '50s, big hair and penny loafers for the '60s, Afros and leisure suits for the '70s. You get the picture. And don't worry about other people's reactions if you go out on the town. You will inspire them to do the same or at least cause them to smile.

After you choose a decade, plan your date around that era. Dress up in the trendy outfits of the day, and don't forget to re-create those fabulous hairstyles. Dance to that decade's greatest hits. Watch a classic movie or a TV series from that decade. (Many stores now sell classic series on DVD.) Be sure to eat the foods specific to your era, too. (For example, if you choose the '50s, eat TV dinners or a homemade tuna casserole at home, or eat at an old-time diner.) Give each other a pop culture quiz. Make out in the backseat of your car!

Before the night is over, be sure to take pictures. You'll want to remember this date for many years.

BUDGET

$-$$ You can save a lot of money on costumes by shopping at thrift stores. You can usually rent classic TV series or movies if you don't want to buy them. And making your own retro meal can save you money.

STEPS TO SUCCESS

- Sit down first and brainstorm. Choose your target decade by secret ballot so you both get to see the other's first choice. If your choices differ, you may have to make this a two-date affair.
- Shop for costumes, movies, music, and food together. Make this prep time part of the date.

OVER THE TOP

- Host a retro party. Enlist the help of friends for planning and preparation.

GET CONNECTED

- If you opt for a '50s night, check out **fiftiesweb.com**.
- Key search words: retro party, '50s themed party, '60s music, food in '70s, '50s food recipes

The greatest
pleasure of life
is love.

SIR WILLIAM TEMPLE

You Pick!

If you haven't done this before, you'll be amazed at how much fun it is. Make a date to go together to a local orchard or berry farm. Choose something you both really like to eat, and be sure to plan carefully. What you take home will have to be dealt with — canned, frozen, served, or given away within a few days or a week at most.

In many parts of the country, you will be able to pick apples, peaches, pears, strawberries, blueberries, cherries, maybe even figs. In some areas, your choices are even broader.

If you aren't feeling up to doing the work yourself, you can buy what you want — already picked by someone else! Most farms also carry jams and jellies, honey, derivative items, juices, and a variety of other fascinating products. You'll go home with smiles on your faces and your arms full of the earth's bounty.

BUDGET

$–$$ Cost is reasonable, even if you don't choose to pick the fruit yourself.

WHAT TO TAKE

- Gardening gloves
- Long-sleeved tops and long pants
- Hat
- Comfortable shoes
- Insect repellent

GET CONNECTED

- Key search words: pick your own blackberries (or whatever fruit you want) followed by your city and state

number
52

Progressive Dinner for Two

What you have in mind is something fun, yet romantic, and it includes a night out for dinner. But it's so difficult to decide where to go. You love the artichoke dip at that little place in town — but you'd also like a good steak, and for that you'll probably want the steak house south of town. What about dessert? Your favorite coffeehouse always has the most decadent one, but they don't serve dinner. So what will you do?

How about going to all those places — in one spectacular evening of favorite food and special places? Drive on over to the place with the yummy artichoke dip and enjoy a great appetizer. They make it just like you like it. Then head to the steak house for your entrée — the main course cooked just right. For dessert, move on to the place that offers the best carrot cake in town or a bubbling fruit cobbler. It's your call.

BUDGET

$$$ The cost of a nice dinner out.

STEPS TO SUCCESS

- Map out your course ahead of time, and call each place for reservations if needed.
- Start with your appetizer as early as 4:30 or 5:00 so you will have the time to leisurely enjoy all courses.
- Stick to the plan. Don't talk yourself out of any of the stops on your schedule.
- Remember to tip at each stop.

OVER THE TOP

- Between dinner and dessert, go dancing. It's a great way to work off those calories, and it's a romantic interlude in your evening.

- Plan to spend the night in a nice hotel, and order dessert to be shared in your room.
- End the evening with a candlelight dessert back home, where you can linger over it as long as you like.

GET CONNECTED

- Check out the menus of your favorite restaurants online.

There is no remedy
for love, but to love more.

HENRY DAVID
THOREAU